Move Over Hot Flashes

Tips For Releasing The Fear And Starting Your Entrepreneurial Journey

Sandra Tatum

Copyright © 2019 by Sandra Tatum

All rights reserved. No part of this publication may be reproduced, distributed, or transmitted in any form or by any means, including photocopying, recording, or other electronic or mechanical methods, without the prior written permission of the publisher, except in the case of brief quotations embodied in critical reviews and specific other noncommercial uses permitted by copyright law...

Are you ready to Release the Fear and Rejection?

Most of what you need is instruction and encouragement from someone who has "been there and had success," and Sandra will do just that! She will also share how rediscovering her inner child gave her confidence in business.

As you can see, releasing fear and rejection in business expert Sandra Tatum is uniquely qualified to help you understand everything you need to know about how gratitude and action helped her overcome her fear and start a profitable business!

She is ready to let you in on a couple of secrets she has learned from her mentors to help you achieve the same success that she has.

Thank you for helping me get over my fears so I could build my agency, and live out my dreams as an entrepreneur!

~Leah Gold Financial Services Consultant/Broker

Table of Contents

Dedications 1

A Special Note About how I Created this Book 3

Chapter 1: Meet Sandra Tatum, Your #1 Releasing Fear And Rejection in Business Expert 5

Chapter 2: Your First Step To Releasing Fear And Rejection in Business 19

Chapter 3: What is One of the Biggest Obstacles You Had to Overcome? 33

Chapter 4: The Next Step To Releasing Fear And Rejection 39

Chapter 5: Critical Advice When Getting Started with Releasing Fear And Rejection. 49

Chapter 6: The Perfect Mindset For Middle-aged Women Interested In Becoming Entrepreneurs 53

Chapter 7: To Truly Release Fear And Rejection, Don't Waste Your Time Doing This 55

Chapter 8: My Secret Tip for Crushing Thoughts of
Fear And Rejection 57

Chapter 9: How Releasing Fear Landed Me Big
Commissions 59

Chapter 10: Why This Epic Fail Was My Proudest
Moment...64

Chapter 11: Do You Really Have a Choice? 68

Chapter 12: Where To From Here… 71

About The Author..72

Dedications

To Mattie and Robert my mom and dad. I thank you for loving and supporting me unconditionally. I thank you for stepping in and helping to take care of my daughter when I was out of town on business.

You continue to inspire me daily to be the best person that I can be in this life. Because of your examples, I know it is my mission to leave the world in a better place than when I arrived.

You have continued to help those who cannot help themselves, even when you knew they were not grateful for your assistance. Thank you for instilling the value of life and what it means to love.

To my husband, my rock and the love of my life. You continue to help me be the best person that I can be. I appreciate your love and support, my Sarge! My beautiful daughter, my Mini-Me, you have taught me how to love unconditionally. I am grateful you have my son (son-in-law) in your life, building a future. I thank you for grounding me. I am a better person because I have my family in my life. I appreciate you all! I am grateful for our "Game Nights!"

Christine Carlo from the moment we first met you believed in me, and you were not shy in letting me now, "you are playing small." I appreciate you being bold and not blowing smoke up my butt. There are no accidents, God put you in my life at the time I needed it the must. You have been and inspiration and supportive beyond belief. I am grateful for your love and support.

Subrira Folami and Zamara Perri thank you for your coaching, mentoring and inspiration. Without you this would not be published today. You continue to bring the best out of so many people. I am grateful for you wanting to share your gifts with the world.

I am grateful for so many more people in my life and in my world, but I had to stop at this point or this book would have been filled with dedication and love only.

A Special Note About how I Created this Book

Dear Sisters Interested In Becoming an Entrepreneur,

Thank you for claiming your copy of "Move Over Hot Flashes: Release the Fear."

This book will teach you critical skills, tools, techniques and more that, every mature woman interested in becoming an entrepreneur, crippled by fear of rejection, needs to understand and apply.

I created this book from a live interview.

That's why it reads like a conversation rather than a traditional "book" that talks "at" you.

I wanted you to feel as though I am talking "with" you, much like the sister I never had, a friend or relative.

Sandra Tatum

I felt that creating the material this way would make it easier for you to grasp the topics and put them to use quickly, rather than wading through hundreds of pages.

So, relax! Get something to write with and take some notes on any and everything that you find useful.

Now get ready to release thoughts of fear and rejection so that you can take your business to the next level.

As a bonus, I will address how rediscovering my inner child gave me confidence in business and can give you the same confidence too!

Let's get started talking about how overcoming my fear led me to start a profitable business right now.

Sincerely,
Sandra Tatum

Chapter 1: Meet Sandra Tatum, Your #1 Releasing Fear And Rejection in Business Expert

Zamara Perry: Hi everyone, and welcome to Move Over Hot Flashes - Release the Fear. My name is Zamara Perri, and today I'm talking with entrepreneur Sandra Tatum.

She's going to share with us how every middle-aged woman interested in becoming an entrepreneur can get started on the right track with releasing fear and rejection so they can obtain business success.

Welcome, Sandra.

Sandra Tatum: Thank you, Zamara. I appreciate you having me.

ZP: Sandra is an expert on the subject of releasing fear and rejection in business, and has graciously consented to this interview.

Sandra Tatum

As a coach and mentor Sandra has helped numerous people release their fears, so they could achieve their goals and move on to have successful professional and financial lives.

Now, her goal with us today is to give us a beginner's guide in this area, so that women who are interested in becoming entrepreneurs at a later age — post hot flashes — can understand how to get started.

She will also share with us how re-discovering her inner child gave her the confidence she needed to move forward in business.

ZP: Again, Sandra, thank you for joining us on this live interview. Let's jump right in.

ST: Thank you.

ZP: My first set of questions are going to be about your background and experience in the area of fear and rejection in business.

I know our audience of older women will be interested in learning how you got over your fear. I know there are a lot of folks who can relate with what you went through.

Sandra Tatum

So, let's start with the first question. Could you tell us a little bit about yourself in terms of your background and experience in dealing with fear and rejection in business?

ST: I basically had a line-in-the-sand moment. That line-in-the-sand moment came after working at a corporate job for over 30 years.

I was doing something that I absolutely loved, but I hadn't gotten a raise in probably ten years. The raises didn't come even though I continued to successfully take on every challenge that was presented to me.

My specialty was training insurance professionals, and I had a lot of success with training various individuals and groups.

At one point, between 2015 and 2017, I had some of the highest-performing teams. Which meant they out outperformed the entire market for California.

When I went to apply for promotions, I was casually rejected. Not because of skills or knowledge, but because I did not live in the right geographical area.

The corporate rating system for performance was based on a scale of one (1) through three (3), with 3 being the highest rating. I consistently received a 3/3 performance rating year after year.

ST: I started talking to some of my most trusted mentors and asking for their advice.

Finally, one of them said, "You know what, Sandra, it's time for you to choose "YOU" and stop selling yourself short. You are training everyone above you, cleaning up all of the mistake's others make. You can be quiet and never question anything else. But all I will say is you are being used, the company is not ever going to promote you. You are not in your thirties (30s) and willing relocate every other year."

I was stunned and confused, I asked, "What do you mean?"

She responded, "You're too smart for this."

This was the first time I really looked at myself differently.

This also wasn't the first-time others recognized my intelligence or my work habits. I had other people tell me that I was smart and still others who admired how I made things happen.

Sandra Tatum

So, I started looking online for possible things I could do to make a change in my life. I ran across a bald-headed guy from Hawaii, named Keala Kanae.

He absolutely changed my life.

The training I got from Keala and his team was just unbelievable. He was the real deal.

Part of the training is a list of Personal Development books that are suggested reading and/or audio listening on a daily basis. Some of the books on the list I had already read but decided to read them again.

As I began reading the books for a second time, it was if I had never seen the words before, or even heard of the concepts. That, only solidified for me it was time to make a change. I continue reading daily.

ZP: Wow.

ST: Yeah. I had to start thinking about things differently.

ZP: So, let's back up a little bit. You are now pretty confident because you went ahead and started your own business. But tell me, you kind of hinted that the training changed your life.

Sandra Tatum

Was this the training that helped you release fear and rejection or did you learn it somewhere else? Did you teach yourself? How did you do it?

ST: Confidence is something I had in the financial services and insurance world, because I just love helping people. Especially older people. People around me professionally would not know that I really am an introverted person who likes to just do things by myself.

I believe that my generation of women were taught to be reserved, lady-like and to serve men.

I can remember, asking to go to a house party back in the late 1970s on a Saturday night, only to be told, no! When I would ask, why it was ok for my brother who was only one year old than me at the time to go to the same party, I was always told, it was because he was a boy.

So, I would settle for riding along with my mom to go pick up my brother from the parties later on that same night. While my mom waited in the car, I would go in and dance for one song and then let my brother know we were waiting for him in the car.

Sandra Tatum

Some would say, I have always been confident. But I would say, I did not see myself that way at all.

After being introduced to Keala Kanae, and his team the information they provided helped me to open my eyes to the bigger picture of what could be in my future.

Yes, I learned affiliate marketing, but more importantly, I learned a different mindset.

What I learned from this gentleman, at its core, was mindset training.

This was my foundation. I had to understand what my highest values were because until I realized what my highest values were, I could not even begin to think of being successful at something else.

I had poured my life into a company because I wanted to and it was and still is a great company, but it was time for me to move on and live out my purpose. My purpose has always been helping other people. That is truly my calling.

During the time when my daughter was small and learning how to walk, I missed her first steps, because I was out of town for business. Until now I have suppressed all of those memories, and just did whatever I had to do to keep a smile on my face, and thought that was just the way life was.

It's interesting that it took an affiliate marketing training to help me come face to face with what was really important to me.

ZP: So, give me some of the experiences you've had with releasing fear of rejection in business that may be relevant to the women in our audience who are middle-aged and interested in becoming entrepreneurs.

Then also let's talk a little bit about how you actually overcame that fear to start a profitable business. Give me an example of an experience where the mindset kind of kicked in?

ST: I needed first to understand, "I am worthy." I had to also, understand, "I am lovable, I am unstoppable and I'm capable of all things."

One of the clearest memories I had was sharing information about a product I was marketing with a potential client.

They accused me of scamming them.

Sandra Tatum

I found myself going back and forth with them on Facebook.

I found myself frantically trying to explain, "No, no, no, no, no. I am not scamming you. That's not what it is."

Then I had to remind myself, "Wait a minute, everyone has an opinion about everything, and of course, if they don't understand it, that's okay."

I had to go back to my childhood because as children, we had no fear. At least, I didn't.

As a child, my nickname was "Puney."

I got the name because I was a little daredevil! I would follow my brothers up to the roof of my almost two-level house and jump off!

I literally channeled my inner Puney and had to go back and summon that same courage I had as a child.

This was the same courage that allowed me to take a good, long hard look at my life.

I was in my mid-fifties, married for more than 30 years and mother to a to a beautiful daughter. What example am I leaving for her and the rest of my family.

I had kept my head down while working in the same industry that rewards designations and people who are mobile.

I elected to not apply for promotions if it meant I had to relocate to another state. That was my choice to not disrupt my family. However, once my daughter finished high school and went off to college, I did apply and continued to be passed over. I needed to change something.

I needed another opportunity!

But first, I had to release my fear and my anxiety.

"You are the same person who jumped off the roof as a kid," I reminded myself.

"Now you need to get in here and do this new thing! You need to understand you're doing this because you need to move on and find a place where you can earn an income, without working 10 – 12 hours a day without a raise for 10 years.

Sandra Tatum

ST: I needed to control my own income. So, I started reading *The 4-Hour Workweek*, a book by Tim Ferriss, to help me put some basic principles in place.

When I read the book and started putting those principles in place, things started clicking for me.

One of the first things I tried to do as an affiliate marketer was to share my story through a Facebook post. But I couldn't get it to work.

I was still new to Facebook and found myself getting frustrated.

All I wanted was for people to know a little bit of my story.

But then, I decided to stop, take a deep breath and remind myself, who I was!

So, I went back and rewrote my story. I chose to tell it in a different way on Facebook.

Just like that, this new version of my story successfully posted and got a lot of attention!

Facebook then approached me and asked me if I wanted to run that as an ad from my post.

Sandra Tatum

I'm like, "What? Wait. Huh? [chuckle] Really? It's just my story." I was so happy and so proud.

One of the things my mentors, Keala Kanae, Ray Kakuda, DMarco Musa, and Jeff Sclafani will always say, "we are so close, and we don't realize how close we are to just changing our lives in an instant."

By telling our stories, someone else will be able to benefit from it.

I told myself, "Okay, alright. Well, you're having these hot flashes, just step back, drink some ice-cold water and fan yourself. You have a story to tell and someone will want to hear it"

[laughter]

ZP: Well, I do want to come back a little bit to that experience you had with the person who said you were scamming them. It's interesting, because sometimes the opinion of a person that you don't even know can sometime affect you.

ST: Yes, that is quite true!

ZP: Even though you know yourself, and you know that you're providing a quality product and your job is really to connect consumers with a quality product,

Sandra Tatum

people sometimes feel offended that you are getting paid for your expertise.

ST: True. But I remember everything my grandmother would say about opinions and that is, everyone has an opinion, and everyone also has an a-hole. So, I just move forward, but you have to learn to let things go, and I can now...

[laughter]

ST: As you get older, you realize that those are small things. My objective is to go out and make this world better than when I arrived!

ZP: Awesome. So, did this happen for you overnight? We're talking about fear and fear of rejection here!

After you started being a part of this community, did you get it overnight or did it take a little bit longer?

ST: So, I didn't even belong to Facebook before joining this community. But, no it did not happen for me overnight. However, I will tell you that it happened quickly.

I truly attribute my success to my mindset. I started to change my thoughts. I changed the way I spoke about myself, to myself and to others. I remember reading a book written by Dr. Wayne Dyer, "Wishes Fulfilled," it stated, "Anytime you start a sentence with I AM you are creating what you are and what you want to be."

I started doing daily affirmations. I also took action with what I said I was going to do.

I kept my promises to myself.

I wrote down my goals, and I read them daily.

ZP: Sandra, let's pause for a minute. You said your success in your new business venture happened quickly.

You're hitting on a fear that some folks have, that they're going to spend years struggling before they can turn a profit in their business because a lot of companies fail.

ST: Right. You're absolutely right.

Chapter 2
Your First Step To Releasing Fear And Rejection in Business

ZP: I feel that you're the right person to talk about how women can release their fear of rejection in business.

So, what is the first step, in your opinion, that women who are experiencing fear and rejection wanting to become entrepreneurs should do?

What's the first step that they need to take with releasing fear and rejection when it comes to starting a business?

You also promised you'd share more about how staying in a state of gratitude and taking action helped you overcome your fears and start your business.

ST: So, for me, the first step was getting back to that place of gratitude and making sure that each day, I spoke to Sandra. I spoke to Sandra in the mirror in the morning.

I look at myself and say, "I am great. I am worthy. I am lovable. I am capable. I am powerful. I am a new me. I am creative."

I always say, thank you for allowing me to be creative and that "I am successful."

Then I remind myself of the abundance of the universe and there is no scarcity in this world, there is enough for all of us.

Finally, I researched businesses, related jobs and things I could do whether online or at another financial service/insurance company. That is how I came across Keala Kanae.

Well, what you don't know is that, in my former corporate job, I also had training on investigating fraud.

ZP: Really?

ST: Yes. So, I knew, then, I needed to research the company associated with Keala Kanae thoroughly. The only thing that people could say bad about this company was that, well, it's a little more expensive, but nothing bad could be said about it and/or the man, Keala Kanae.

Keala is the real deal. Keala wants success for others, more than you want it for yourself.

So, I knew I was on to something. His emphasis on continuing education appealed to me. So, I dove in!

ZP: So okay, you said a couple of things, but let's kind of focus on the first step. Remind me again, did you say the first step was gratitude?

ST: For me, it was gratitude. Gratitude and affirmations.

ZP: Tell me more.

ST: I had to completely go into Sandra, understanding that Sandra can do this.

ZP: Okay. So why is it essential that this is the first step? Or that this was the first step for you?

ST: I had to be able to get out of my own way, get myself back into a place of believing in me and understanding I am worthy, and once I understood that, the universe takes care of everything else.
The same thing can happen to you as long as:

- you're taking action;
- staying in that state of gratitude;
- knowing your purpose;
- your why; and
- wanting the good for you and everyone else around you!

ZP: What is the best way to get started with a gratitude and affirmation practice?

ST: I believe you should consider reading the book, The Magic, by Rhonda Byrnes. The book sets out, step-by-step for you, things that you can do to bring yourself back into a state of gratitude. It recommends you start journaling daily.

I journal every single morning what I am grateful for that day, what I am thankful for in the past, what I am thankful for in the present, what is coming, even if it has not happened yet. I am setting the intention. This is a daily practice that helps to put me in a positive mood.

I have also written out the goals I want to accomplish in 30, 60, and 90 days. I sent my goals to my accountability partner and Sister from another mother Sina Suemoto.

Sandra Tatum

I needed a strong female who would call me out if she saw me not doing what I said I was going to do. Sina is that person for me. I appreciate her more than she can ever imagine.

I read my goals, reaffirm and check them off as the goal is achieved. I continually reinvent my goals.

The number one thing about goal setting is—your goals should always be so scary when you read them, and if it's not, those aren't the right goals for you.

You want to be able to achieve them, and the universe has it all for you.

Some people may be a little bit more confused about me referring to the universe. Some people call it "spirit or God." I believe in God!

When I think about it, I believe comedian D. L. Hughley said it best for me.

He said, "In religion we call it spirits. In science we call it energy. In the streets we call it vibes. All I'm saying is trust it."

If you want success in any area you must have goals. Must people don't ever achieve what they want in life, it is not because they are not capable, it not because they lack opportunity, it's not because of the circumstances which arrive in their lives. Most often we do not define what we want in life.

In a recent study, it was found that less than three (3) percent of population set goals. Only 3 percent have some direction in life. Why?

If you do not have goals you will never achieve your dreams. But you will continue to work building someone else's dreams and fulfilling their goals. You must consider the following when working on your goals:

- Write your goals down!
- You must be specific!
- Know exactly what you want out of life!
- Find clarity quickly!
- Learn how you are going to get what you want!
- Learn with a purpose!
- Focus on context-based learning!
- If there is already a blue-print follow it!
- Work until you do get it!
- Read your goals DAILY!
- Consistency!
- Allow your goals to sink into your subconscious mind.

Sandra Tatum

If your goals are easy to achieve, they are not big enough! Your goals must be scary and exciting all at the same time!

Breakdown your goals into easy actionable steps. Take action and build momentum.

Define your REASON WHY. Find a deep emotional reason why you cannot give up on your goals. It must be a reason so great that you will not give up.
If you want success in any area of your life you must have goals. It will give you a reason to live and stretch yourself.

ZP: One of the things that people often want to know when they're trying to establish something new, like setting goals, a gratitude practice or affirmation practice, is what tools or websites or maybe apps should they use?

ST: Oh, there are multiple apps out there, whether it's on Android or iOS, meaning Apple.

Just put in "gratitude," in the search bar. Some apps will have periodic reminders for you to pause and be grateful.

Sandra Tatum

There are gratitude apps for personal, business, money or health. It just depends on what you need.

But I genuinely believe you need to first look at yourself to figure out what you need in your life at this time.

If you don't know, turn to your spouse, best girlfriend, mother, sister, friend, someone who you trust and tell them how you're feeling.

Then ask, "What do you think I need? What do you see in me that I don't see in myself?"

The people who genuinely love you see you very differently than you see yourself because you are harder on yourself than you need to be.

When it comes to setting goals consider this:

Too often, people give up on their dreams because their goals seem far too unattainable. For example, those living on a low income could dream of becoming a millionaire, but quickly give up on the idea as they believe that it is simply impossible.

But, is it? Many low-earning, average people have beat the odds and become hugely successful, even famous.

Each of these people have one secret in common: A successful mind-set.

How to Build Goals

Take a moment to really think about yourself and the way in which you approach things.

Do you quickly give up on goals that you deem impossible to reach?

Does the idea of working for a long period of time to achieve a goal fill you with feelings of dread? Are you quick to give up if something doesn't happen soon enough, or do you have the patience to wait and persevere?

If, like many people, you prefer instant or at least quick gratification, setting smaller goals to build up to one main goal is the best strategy for you.

Setting small, achievable goals as 'building blocks' to a larger achievement is a method for success that works tremendously well for many people. This method allows you to break down the amount of work that you need to do to achieve your goals into smaller, more manageable portions.

Rather than setting one goal of 'start a business', setting several smaller goals which, by achieving each one, will eventually prepare you to become a business owner can help to put things into perspective.

There's a reason why this method is commonly used by people who are hoping to lose a lot of weight, for example. Let's say that you are overweight and need to lose 100 lbs. – taking on the whole amount at once can be massively overwhelming.

Example: What if you break it down to ten weight loss goals of 10 lbs. each? Suddenly, it becomes much easier to manage and goal attainment does not seem as impossibly so far away.

Strategic Goal Setting

Dividing your goal into multiple, smaller and more easily achievable goals is often one of the best ways to achieve success. But, in order to attain the end results that you want, it's important to have the right strategy. Making sure that you set the right goals which will lead up to your end goal is hugely important.

For this reason, this goal setting task is not one which should ever be rushed. The more thought and effort that you put into designing and setting your goals, the better your result will be.

For example, if your main goal is to buy a home, don't just set yourself savings goals. Instead, set goals that cover everything that is needed to eventually purchase a property – for example this could include improving your credit limit or even researching areas to live.

Once you're finally able to buy a home, you will find that the more you have achieved beforehand, the easier it will be. Let's not forget that the more you consciously decide to do, the better programmed your subconscious mind will become.

Setting Time Limits

One of the biggest mistakes that many people make is to set time limits for their goals. While sometimes this can be unavoidable, if possible, it's always best to ensure that you have as much time as you need to achieve your goal, or at the very least set yourself a reasonable time limit. Giving yourself too little time to achieve your goal can result in your stress levels rising, causing you to make rash decisions and even damaging your mental well-being. When setting a goal which needs a time limit, giving yourself the maximum amount of time available is key to keeping your stress levels to a minimum.

On the other hand, certain people may find that time limits motivate them and encourage them to be proactive. If you fall into this category, working out reasonable time limits for each of your goals may be the best way for you to approach them.

However, when using this strategy, it's crucial that you do not fall into the trap of believing that you have failed if you fail to achieve a goal with in the designated time frame.

When working towards goals with time limits, it's important to keep close track of your progress in order to determine in advance whether you think you can meet the time deadline or not. When possible, extending your time limit should always be considered if you believe that it is needed.

Remember that going at your own pace and understanding that life is unpredictable is vital.

ZP: I think you answered my next question! One of my questions was going to be, what happens when you get stuck on this step? So, you're recommending having your family and friends speak life into you?

Sandra Tatum

ST: Yes, absolutely! You'd be surprised at how they can see you probably as that strong, solid individual that's always showing up for everyone else.

But you have to remember to show up for yourself, and believe in you, first and foremost.

There is a reason why on an airplane the Flight Attendant will ask you to put on your oxygen mask first, then the child and/or other person you are with.

Because if your cup is truly empty, you can't fill anyone else's cup. Being in a state of gratitude and in grace, your cup will stay full. Which will allow you to automatically want to fill the cups of others who are around you.

ZP: I like that a lot. Now, you've had a pretty tough past. Did it take you a long time to get to the point where you could do a daily gratitude journal and release that fear of rejection?

And how did you know that it was working?

ST: I have always been a very positive person. But, I needed to be around like-minded people, who wanted to make positive changes. So I would say it took me approximately 60 days or so to shift my mindset.

I knew it was working because of what I saw instantaneously. It started in my marriage. I saw the communication changed between me and the man who I have been married to for over thirty (30) years!

I could communicate with him, and before, I think I was talking at him as opposed to talking with him.

I understood some of the things he was trying to say to me, and get this, Zamara, he believed in me so much, but I couldn't hear it before!

He's always told me very positive things about me, but I didn't want to hear it! I cannot tell you how many times he told me to quit working at the corporate job, because he knew there was something else, I was supposed to be doing, but I never wanted to listen.

I was so trapped in the baggage I had. Unfortunately, I'm sure I saddled him with a lot of my baggage. So, I thank God he saw something in me and continued to be by my side.

Chapter 3
What is One of the Biggest Obstacles You Had to Overcome?

ST: I went through a process of not only learning about affiliate marketing, but I learned more about myself.

I had so much stuff going on that goes back to my childhood that I did not even know what was getting in my way.

Working through those childhood issues and constantly reading helped me to rediscover the real me.

ST: One of the biggest traumas I suffered, happened to me at the age of ten (10).

I was living in the Los Angeles area. On this particular day, everyone on our block left to go to a young man's funeral services., who had committed suicide. I wasn't feeling that well, so I stayed home by myself.

Sandra Tatum

When I went outside to sit on the porch, a young man from our neighborhood was passing by.
He came over and said, "Hey, why didn't you go to the service?"

I told him that I didn't feel that well.

He then asked, "Oh, can I have some water?"

So, knowing I wasn't supposed to have anyone in the house, I still said, "Okay."

Even though he lived just a few houses down the street, I went into my house to get the water. Little did I know he was going to come into the house, I thought he would wait on the porch. The nightmare began, he tried to rape me in my kitchen.

ZP: Wow.

ST: I remember that he ripped my blouse and tried to take advantage of me. I am not sure how but I managed to get my hands on a cast iron skillet and I tried to beat the hell out of him with that skillet.

I can only say my angels protected me that day, and I am so thankful for my mama's skillet.

Sandra Tatum

ZP: Wow.

ST: The skillet and my angels were the only thing that saved me from being raped.

In my mind, it was my fault because I was not supposed to have anyone in the house. I had nightmares for years.

Years after almost being raped, when men hollered at me on the street, I would just panic.

I could not tell my mother what happened because of the fear that I would get in trouble for not listening and following the house rules, "no one is allowed in the house unless my parents where home."

So, I kept that in for a very long time.

Finally, at the age of 40, I told my mother what happened.

My mother is a loving mom, she just looked in shock, and said, "I am your mother, and you can tell me anything. I am sorry if I made you feel anything differently."

That experience of almost being raped started me down the path of telling myself stories to survive.

Sandra Tatum

One of the most common stories that women tell ourselves is that it's harder for women in the corporate world.

While it is, I can guarantee you that we find a way to get whatever it is that we have been assigned to do, done.

Women make things happen so we can take care of our families. It has been done for generations.

But even with that being said, so many of us still have a sense of failure, because we missed our children growing up. The early years. Their first steps, or we were busy working while our children were at their track meets, their basketball games, their volleyball games, their baseball games, etc.

We as women harbor so much, and we've got to learn to let it go and learn that there is a whole new world out there.

The world is changing so that we can stay home and not have to work all those hours and earn even more income than we could ever imagine!

ZP: Well, thank you so much for sharing that story. I'm glad that you were able to fight him off, and I'm happy that you were able to let that go because of course, carrying that around for 30 years, that impacts your self-esteem and your relationships, and your success.

ST: Absolutely! But I attribute it, again to that ad from Keala Kanae and getting into the various training sessions that allowed me to pursue the laptop lifestyle. Allowing me to work for myself, work remotely for an employer and/or as a freelancer. It's not just affiliate training; it's much, much more than that.

ZP: So, can people come to you for training especially since you've seen the results of the training yourself?

ST: Absolutely! I would also encourage them to go beyond that and move forward into some advanced training, which is a part of business model Mr. Kanae has established.

The programs take you from awakening your mind. To activating your subconscious and then accelerating your success.

There are a host of programs that will guide you step-by-step. It is a lifetime of training, and along the way you will meet various mentors that will assist you in whatever you need to catapult your success.

Sandra Tatum

When you don't believe in yourself, they encourage you to call them and talk about what's happening.

So, if I'm not available, they're available, and there's a whole community of people who are there to answer your questions. You can step back and reach out to another person in the community, because someone knows the answer to the question, and if they do not, they know who does.

Chapter 4
The Next Step To Releasing Fear And Rejection

ZP: That's wonderful. So, what is the second step that women who are at this point in their life need to take in order to release their fear of rejection and run a profitable business from home?

ST: I think you have to get into a community of like-minded people and build a bond.

During my time with Keala Kanae, I learned the importance of continually training, mindset and goal setting.

I also belonged to a community of like-minded individuals. We have a Facebook community where we always cheer each other on.

We also have with in the communities' mastermind groups.

Sandra Tatum

Even that person who may be an introvert, who may not want to go and network in person, can choose to network online now.
In doing my work, some folks in the London area came across me on Facebook.

They saw some of the posts I was posting about mindset and gratitude, and one of the founders of a domestic violence organization in London reached out to me.

I've wanted to start a foundation for domestic violence survivors as well as for at-risk youth, because of some of the things that I had come across as a young child. I've always done a lot of volunteer work to support at-risk youth and domestic violence survivors.

So here it was, the universe had put me in touch with someone who shared my same mission and passion!

ST: She's already doing the things in London that I'd like to do in the United States and is very successful at it.

So just by simply joining in various communities, I connected with a person who's built her business using a different platform, a different model, but she's also doing the actual foundation work that I would like to do.

She's been very instrumental in teaching me what is working for her over there, and the success of programs that she already has in place. So, the key here is that networking and joining communities is huge.

ZP: So how do you get into finding community and networking?

ST: You start putting in keyword searches on Facebook, or keyword searches into Google.

ZP: When you say "keyword searches," what does that mean?

ST: So, for me, that means searching for groups I could relate to. So, I searched for terms like "working women" or insurance affiliates."

Various groups come up. Each group on Facebook has information about their purpose, where they are located, how many people are in their actual group, what it takes to join and what the expectations are.

Sandra Tatum

I would suggest as you search the numerous groups to find ones that resonates with you and then ask to join.

If it's a fit, stay in, at that point you get active in responding and answering questions or posing questions. You may find someone who lives very close by you, and then you can join a local group.

ST: When the community I am involved in has a live event, some people will join up together and look for roommates.

Let's say there's an event in Las Vegas. Instead of staying in hotels, they'll do an Airbnb inside of a large home. A lot of times, you can be there for four, five days and some people will only spend $43 a night ... and they have the run of a huge mansion.

This is all because they've joined a network and/or community.

ZP: That's awesome.

ST: They also share cars and/or share transportation to save time and money. That way, you're not at an event by yourself.

If you're in the house with others you are able to get their perspective on what was presented at the event and how they may take advantage of building out another revenue source.

You're learning from each other what's working in their business, things you'd like to implement, as you build long-term relationships.

ZP: So, it sounds like you're saying that, for folks who are interested in finding community, really Facebook is a major place to find that community.
ST: Absolutely!

ZP: Are there any other websites or apps, for folks who are not necessarily Facebook savvy or other options for meeting folks offline that you've experienced?

ST: There are some women's organizations that are local. I suggest also looking into AARP. They have various networking organizations for people wanting to work after retirement

So, for most people, retirement age is 62 to 67 1/2. But some people are not necessarily able to make that retirement age. Some companies are downsizing and calling it "right-sizing" or moving to other locations.

Sandra Tatum

ST: So, you may have companies from California moving to Nevada, Arizona, or Texas, for major business hubs, and tax benefits.

Well, some of their people are being layed off right before retirement.

So, there are different outreach programs to help them adjust to a new reality.

You also have some outreach programs through churches. You can also find support targeting older workers even through the unemployment resource service, Employment Development Departments in your state of domicile.

So those are things that people can consider too if they don't have Internet access.

I would always encourage anyone to go to a local library and utilize the free Wi-Fi and computer until they are more familiar with computers.

ZP: Okay, so if someone gets stuck in the networking part of the process, how do they even get out of being trapped?

Sandra Tatum

You will need to treat your relationship building like a business. Start to think about networking like the following:

- Give before you ask. (Be willing to give your time to help with an event to learn the planning process. Then the person may be more willing to assist you.)
- Figure out who matters most.
- Think people not positions or what you can get from the connection.

Is there a tip that you have for getting people to see the value in networking and changing their mindset to appreciating it more?

ST: Most people who are successful want to help others be just as successful as they are and love to share their knowledge. They simply want to give back to support other. So you should network to learn to follow the blueprint of other successful people, it will be an easier path and you will see success sooner.

If you have children and/or grandchildren, I would suggest asking them about communities on Facebook.

Sandra Tatum

So I found that when you find something that is truly important to you, you get excited about supporting others.

When you realize that you can impart knowledge on a 25-year-old and then that same 25-year-old person can impart knowledge on you, you find the value in that, so you become much more willing connect.

When you realize a person has the same mindset as you, you will spend your time talking to them for hours. Because you appreciate the value the person brings to your life.

ST: One of the things that was important for me was connecting with people in my local area.

I went on a retreat sponsored by a company headed by Todd Campbell and Keala Kanae. During the retreat, I was able to face some of my biggest fears and release them. Remember, you have to learn techniques to deal with your fears and limited mindset, so you can know each day how to deal with it and move on.

During my time at the retreat I continued my journaling practice to manifest meeting people locally in my community. I just got up earlier to make sure I continued with my journaling on a daily basis.

Sandra Tatum

As it turned out, with in a 30-mile radius, there were five people that were living in southern California and we didn't even know that we lived so close together.

We are looking to collaborate on projects together. It has been really nice to have my intention set and then have liked minded people right in my back yard.

ST: Now, we have become the best of friends, like family.

When one of us is stuck on something, we reach out to each other, and then we meet up to talk about daily habits of keeping our minds right through all the craziness that's going on in this world.

It is one of the most grateful, gracious things that we can do.

When one person has a different idea on something, we talk it out. We help that person frame and research it. We get back together, to discuss how the person can build upon the next business idea.

ZP: All right now. So, it sounds like Keala Kanae and his company has been an excellent group for helping you accelerate your business mindset.

Sandra Tatum

ST: His company is a great place to start. I am also affiliated with other organizations, I believe in multiple streams of income.

Working with Keala Kanae has been so amazing. So much so that I never would have thought someone would come to me and ask me to create actual content to train people with in their business, and then pay me $10,000 for it, ok I will take it!
But I must admit, I was still a little afraid of cashing the check, because I could not believe it was happening!

I have elected for the checks to be mailed and mot use the electronic deposit option, because I like to hold the checks in my hands.

Sandra Tatum

Chapter 5
Critical Advice When Getting Started with Releasing Fear And Rejection.

ZP: I love it. I love it. It sounds awesome. So, we talked about the different ways that middle-aged women who are interested in becoming entrepreneurs can release their fear of rejection when starting a business.

You've said it's through mindset, meditation, gratitude, training and community.

What is that next step that would help them release fear of rejection, take action, and become more confident in the business world?

ST: You need a mentor. If they don't have a mentor, and cannot necessarily voice it, then journal it. Journal it, journal it, journal it!

Sandra Tatum

A lot of people are not comfortable talking to people. So, consider writing down your thoughts, until you get more comfortable and get more reassured.

Then it starts to flow. I guarantee you if you start on the path of gratitude, you set yourself up to take action and believe there is nothing that can stop you from doing exactly what you want, as long as you understand what your highest values are. "Skies the Limit."

ST: Now, you're going to have to do some work. Dr. John Demartini has a wonderful website (https://drdemartini.com/) that can help you to understand your highest values, and he has a book, "The Values Factor." This will help you understand more about yourself and what is important to you. Our values change overtime. So, this is not a one-time evaluation.

Once you understand, you know that there is nothing that will stop you.

ZP: Can you share a little more encouragement with those women who are still in the workforce and not sure they have what it takes to run their own businesses?

Sandra Tatum

ST: While you are working for someone else and building their dreams, you've been stuck working 10 to 12 hours a day. Do you want to continue building someone else's dreams?

When it comes to your own business, you will, in fact, want to work that hard for you because you understand the payoff, and you will not have to work consistently for 60 hours a week to obtain those same results. Find and understand your purpose, make sure your "WHY" makes you excited and nervous all at the same time.

The results will be so much sweeter, because as you start to learn, grow and build, you will see your biggest problem is the increase in your income. What can I do as far as tax planning? How can I buy this rental property and/or would it be better to put the money in stocks and bonds to continue to build legacy wealth? You will be able to take a vacation when you want to, not when the corporate world approves vacation for you. Your time becomes yours.

ZP: Wow.

ST: Never would I ever have thought I would be able to do that. But I didn't understand my value before.

Sandra Tatum

ZP: So, do you think that having a mentor helped you, or was it just a combination of all these things?

ST: I believe it's a combination of everything! None of this was happening until I got with a specific mentor Keala Kanae and his team, so you can't tell me there's not a connection!

Once I started my gratitude practice, started to understand my highest values, then understanding what I was worth and what I was giving away, people started approaching me.

You can't tell me there's not a correlation there. I still continue to give to others to help them succeed; it's helping me to succeed as well.

Chapter 6
The Perfect Mindset For Middle-aged Women Interested In Becoming Entrepreneurs

ZP: So, tell me ... I know we've talked a little bit about the mindset, and I think you've hit on it, but let's try again to say it concisely.

So what is the perfect mindset for women who are a little bit older, who are middle-aged, perhaps, who are interested in becoming an entrepreneur?

ST: You have to have a mindset that there is nothing that will stop you. You are courageous, you are worthy, and you are capable of all things! You must remember someone is depending on you to be successful, and there is no scarcity in this world. It is our birth right to live an abundant life.

Stop with the negative self-talk. You should be looking in the mirror daily and saying, "Damn, I look good today."

Sandra Tatum

I don't care if you look like crap and you've got rollers all over your hair. You can still say, "I look good today," because you know what?

You do look good. It's just a matter of you going through, combing your hair, washing your face and brushing your teeth. You got this!

ZP: All right now.

ST: The rest is done, 'because remember, you can put lipstick on a pig, and that pig will look good to someone!

[laughter]

Chapter 7
To Truly Release Fear And Rejection, Don't Waste Your Time Doing This

ZP: I have a couple more questions if you don't mind.

ST: Sure.

ZP: You've given us a lot of resources, really, about the mindset, and you've mentioned some books, some websites, but I'm wondering, where do you see women entrepreneurs waste a lot of time?

ST: Unfortunately for women, we wear our emotions on our sleeves, and we have to think more like men from the standpoint of, we can't care what people are thinking about us, we have to get over that, we cannot continue to become so emotional!

As long as you know that you're doing the right thing and living your life with purpose, that's all you have to be concerned with. Build-up that next woman, don't tear them down.

Sandra Tatum

No matter what, get away from all the crap, the he said, she said in the media and gossip. Stick to the facts. My mother would tell us as kids, "if you do not have anything good to say about the person, then don't say anything at all."

When you're on Facebook, you should not be trolling to see what people are talking about or who did this and who did that.

Worry about you. Think about what positive things you can do to build someone up and be a positive influence. Consider mentoring our youth. That's where you're going to get your energy and your fuel.

The rest of that stuff is just crap, and you won't get anything out of it. Quite honestly, it only helps to bring you down and depress you. You want to stay on a positive road trip not the negative one.

Chapter 8
My Secret Tip for Crushing Thoughts of Fear And Rejection

ZP: That's wonderful. Now, where are some big opportunities to release the fear and rejection that many beginner entrepreneurs may benefit from?

ST: Stop saying the words "I can't do it," and stop saying that "it's impossible."

Look at that word "impossible" and turn it into "I'm possible."

You break that word down and keep it very simple.

It's already been done. There are blueprints that are out there, all you must do is get with a mentor and start following the same blueprints that have already been set aside if you choose to take action and move forward to change your life.

Sandra Tatum

I had to step outside of my comfort zone in order to release my stress. I am so grateful I did.

ST: Start your business on the side so you can feel more comfortable. As women we are generally more cautious, we are generally risk-averse.

So, consider starting your business as a "side hustle." This will allow you time to learn and execute slowly, but you will be more comfortable doing so. Especially, if you are the primary bread winner in your household.

Once you start seeing your income grow and it is consistent, then it's time for you to go ahead and put both feet in.

Chapter 9
How Releasing Fear Landed Me Big Commissions

ZP: Right! A couple more questions. So is there a particular story or example that you have that would sum up what we've been talking about?

ST: So I was so fearful in starting in affiliate marketing. I had written my story, but I didn't want to share it. I didn't want to tell anyone. I thought, "Oh well, it could be a little shameful."

And then, all of a sudden, I asked myself, "Why?"

So, I shared my story with one of the leaders of my Facebook group. She lives about 45 minutes away from me.

Her name is Julie Bjorkman, and she is so helpful. She's an absolutely wonderful person and continues to keep the community together.

Sandra Tatum

Now, here's a woman who has three children, including a set of twins. Her little girls are three (3) and then her son is five (5). Julie is doing her thing to build community, she is running mastermind groups, and building out a business. You talk about Wonder Woman, that is truly Julie.

She told me how she could not even speak in public before because she was such an introverted person, and this community has helped her learn, mature and become an entrepreneur.

ST: She's setting up various things and running her business, then working through another ad agency.

She told me her story to encourage me.

Julie, continued to pour out the positive, as she does every Tuesday and Sunday evenings. She will always say, "If I can do these things, you can too! She will offer to proof read your Ad Copy and provide feedback.

I shared my story with Julie and she provided feedback. Her tweaks helped me sell three (3) Kangen alkaline water machines through one of my affiliates. When the commission came in, I was like, "This is real. Oh my God."

Sandra Tatum

ZP: Wow.

ST: I was shocked, but I continued to duplicate the process. That's all you have to do. Follow a blueprint.

ZP: So, tell me something. These days do you think it's easier or harder for women interested in becoming entrepreneurs.

Is it easier to let go of fear and rejection in business than it was for maybe when you started?

ST: I think it's harder because the older we get we tend to have so much more baggage.

I think it's much easier to get out of your own way and release those things when you're younger because you don't have as much experience.

You haven't been told, "No. You can't. You won't. You shouldn't do these things." Your subconscious mind has not been poisoned by all the fear and rejection.

If you go back to your inner child, when you didn't have the fear, the negative talk, you will be able to soar.

Even the most successful people must face setbacks and failures at some point.

Failures and setbacks are a huge part of achieving success, even if they are the opposite of what you are working towards. But it is how you deal with these situations that really matters.

Those who achieve success and meet their goals repeatedly tend to constantly face setbacks head on and deal with failures in a positive manner.

Rather than failing once and giving up, successful people keep on trying, persevering and not allowing downfalls to get the better of them. Fall down six (6) times, get up seven (7).

You may have heard the saying – 'never a failure, always a lesson'. This is the mantra of successful people, the motto that almost everybody who constantly experiences a high level of success lives by. It's true – believing and accepting that you have 'failed' and allowing setbacks to get the better of you is a sure-fire way to never achieve your goals for success. Instead, 'failure' should not be an option, release the fear of failure, and embrace it as a lesson.

Even if things do not go as planned, take every setback as a learning curve, try again, use the

Sandra Tatum

experience and knowledge you now have to make better decisions and put different strategies for success in place.

Anything is possible, but you must have faith in yourself, and it's not easy to have confidence in yourself.

It's easier for us to have faith in other things and people. But you must believe in yourself, more than anyone else.

Once you do, I promise you, everyone will rally around to support you. But you must step out of the shadows. Others will help to push you up.

ZP: So, you said something that kind of struck me, that I hadn't thought of it before--that it's much easier for us to believe in other things than in ourselves.

ST: Absolutely. We need to learn to believe in ourselves first, but we don't.

Chapter 10
Why This Epic Fail Was My Proudest Moment

ZP: So, you touched on the inner child thing. How did getting in touch with your inner child help give you have confidence in business, or did it?

ST: It did! I really started believing that there was nothing that I couldn't do. I was literally having a conversation with the person I was back at the age of five (5).

Back then my mom would get complaints from my teachers stating, "the only problem we have with Sandra is that she likes to answer all of the questions. She needs to let the other children have a chance to answer."

Well as we have discussed when you are told time and time again don't answer questions or don't do whatever, you slow down or stop answering question and will become more introverted.

Sandra Tatum

I have another friend and mentor Guy Monzeglio who would share some of his techniques for meditating and the calming effect it had on him. Guy has this great personality that only wants the best for everyone.

He is a devoted dad who has his priorities correct. But understands the pressures of the world being an active dad, who's highest values are related to his family. So, I knew when he told me about his meditation practice that helped him stay in a state of gratitude. I knew whatever, he shared would be great! He shared his audio files after our discussion and a few tricks, I knew I had the "Right Stuff!"

Wow the mediation helped me to slow down my over active brain. Which allowed me to understand that all those things I continued to tell myself I couldn't do was really just a made-up roadblocks. Somethings I made up and told myself for years.

ZP: You had to go back and get in touch with little Puney who didn't have those problems, didn't have those fears, didn't have those roadblocks.

ST: Yes, I had to go back and be my inner Puney to understand I put up all those roadblocks against myself. No one did that to me, but me!

Sandra Tatum

Unfortunately, society continues to tell kids, "No, you can't do that. You can't have that."

"Oh, don't go there. You'll get hurt," or "Oh, don't jump off of there. You're going to get hurt."

Well, when I jumped off the roof, which was almost a two-story building, I didn't get hurt. We would land in the grass laugh and drink water from the water hose.

I didn't get hurt, because I didn't have any fear of getting hurt.

But I recently went through something also, where I was doing some training at a retreat to release some fear.

It involved me climbing up logs and walking across high wires. I slipped, luckily for me my harness held me dangling in the air!

The trainers said, "Well, we're going to bring you down!"

And I responded, "The hell you are!"

[laughter]

Sandra Tatum

"You're not bringing me down. I'm taking myself down, but I'll be coming down."

ST: I yelled down and saw one of the people that I'd like to say is my brother now, Tim Parsons.
I yelled out, "What do I do? How do I get across here now that I have slipped off the wire?"

Because I didn't have the arm strength to pull myself back up, he guided me to the next area to be able to climb up and then walk over to safety.

Even though I slipped off the wire, I am most proud that I still managed to complete the task on my terms.

Chapter 11
Do You Really Have a Choice?

ZP: That is so awesome! As we wrap up, Sandra, is there anything that you want to add to help motivate women who are interested in becoming entrepreneurs, but may be paralyzed by fear?

ST: So, I would say, "Do you really have a choice?"

As we recognize the world is changing with pension plans going away and 401-K plans not being funded we have to think about our future differently.

People are being released or severed from their jobs before they can retire with health insurance, or with their actual pensions in place, do you really want to miss a chance to be in control of your life and your income? Do you want to continue to limit your abilities, or do you want to continue to work 60 hours a week and limit your income?

Consider investing in yourself. You can consider joining a similar community as the one started by my mentor Keala Kanae. I would say, "Go somewhere, do something."

Sandra Tatum

We talk about stores downsizing, re-allocating their resources, shutting down the brick and mortars.

The way that we purchase things, has changed, and it's going to continue to evolve.

People are looking for convenience, most things can be purchased online and delivered to your home. Take advantage and get involved to find your niche' to build your business. People are buying things on the Internet. Why not be a part of it?

ZP: Well, thank you, Sandra, for this great interview.

I'm so sure that all of the women in our audience interested in becoming entrepreneurs have a much better, clearer understanding of how to release those thoughts of fear and rejection in business, and just go for it, just because you've laid it out so clearly.

Thank you so much for sharing your expertise and experiences so graciously.

Thank you to all the women in our audience for joining us for this fantastic beginner's guide conversation.

Sandra Tatum

ST: Thank you.

Chapter 12
Where To From Here...

If you would like to contact Sandra you may do so by going to her website www.thesandratatum.com.

You can email Sandra at Sandra@moveoverhotflashes.com.

If you are interested in receiving bonus tools please go to www.thesandratatum.com to sign-up for her newsletter in regards to *Not Giving Up on Yourself*.

ABOUT THE AUTHOR

Sandra Tatum is an expert in releasing fear and rejection in business whose accomplishments include but not limited to:

Awards, Titles, and Designations:

- Transformational Coach and Mentor;
- Excellence in Operational Management Coach;
- Insurance Professional for 30 years;
- Chartered Life Underwriters (CLU);
- Chartered Financial Consultant (ChFC);
- Associate in Claims (AIC);
- Associate in General Insurance (AINS);
- Workers Compensation Claims Administration (WCCA);
- Master Certified Special Arbitrator;
- Certified Property Subrogation Arbitrator;
- Certified Special Arbitrator - Auto Liability; and
- Certified Special Arbitrator - General Liability

Sandra Tatum

Work History:

- Repeatedly surpassed insurance goals and service levels;
- Trained over 100 inexperienced people to become the highest performing and productive team in the organization; and
- Eliminated waste, driving results and receiving positive customer feedback internally and externally.

Personal Info:

- Married for 30-plus years;
- Mother of an adult daughter;
- Almost raped at the age of 10 by her 18-year-old neighbor;
- Four-figure affiliate marketer with in first quarter of starting her business;
- Five-figure training contracts
- Enjoys writing in her Gratitude Journal every morning; and
- Enjoys playing "Uno" the card game with her family.

www.ingramcontent.com/pod-product-compliance
Lightning Source LLC
Chambersburg PA
CBHW030940240526
45463CB00015B/861